Deer Hunting with Daddy

Written by
Jeanna Johnston

Illustrated by
Patricia Parks

Copyright © 2013 by Jeanna Johnston. 116882-JOHN

Library of Congress Control Number: 2012916076
ISBN: Softcover 978-1-4931-0707-0
  EBook   978-1-4931-0708-7

All rights reserved. No part of this book may be reproduced or transmitted in any form or by any means, electronic or mechanical, including photocopying, recording, or by any information storage and retrieval system, without permission in writing from the copyright owner.

Rev. date: 10/01/2013

To order additional copies of this book, contact:
Xlibris LLC
1-888-795-4274
www.Xlibris.com
Orders@Xlibris.com

Patricia Clifton Parks is a wife and mother of two sons. She received her BFA and Masters of Art in Art from the University of Oklahoma. After teaching in a community college for thirteen years she directed the Art Program for the Lake County School Systems. An avid horsewoman, she now devotes her time to her artwork and her other interests. She lives on the family farm in Ridgely, Tennessee with her husband, Steve and their horses and dogs.

Kids, look for the hidden deer in each picture!

We wake up bright and early before the rooster even crows.

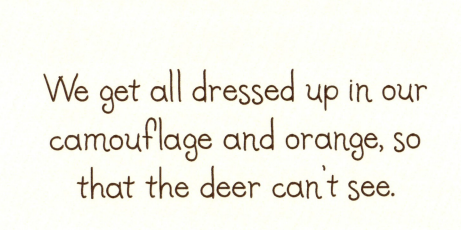

We get all dressed up in our camouflage and orange, so that the deer can't see.

Next, we climb up into our favorite hunting tree.

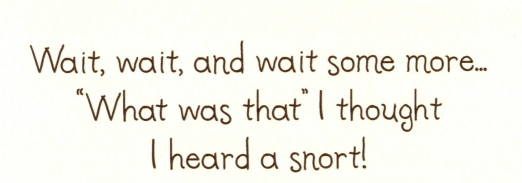

Wait, wait, and wait some more...
"What was that" I thought
I heard a snort!

Out comes a buck with antlers to the sky!

Then, I see Daddy's gun start to rise.

Closer and closer here he comes....

Daddy's got him sighted in his gun!

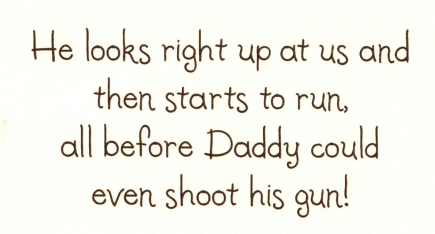

He looks right up at us and
then starts to run,
all before Daddy could
even shoot his gun!

Made in the USA
Monee, IL
13 December 2019